# Guitar

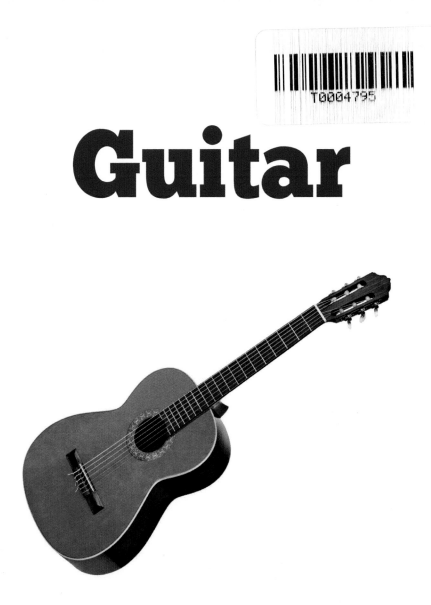

Matilda James

xïst Publishing

## A Note to Parents & Teachers—

Welcome to Discover Musical Instruments from Xist Publishing! These books are designed to inspire discovery and delight in the youngest readers. Each short book features very simple sentences with visual cues to get kids reading for the first time.

You can help each child develop a lifetime love of reading right from the very start. Here are some ways to help a beginning reader get going:

📖 Read the book aloud as a first introduction

📖 Run your fingers below the words as you read each line

📖 Give the child the chance to finish the sentences or read repeating words while you read the rest.

📖 Encourage the child to read aloud every day!

Published in the United States by
Xist Publishing
www.xistpublishing.com
PO Box 61593 Irvine, CA 92602

eISBN: 978-1-5324-1670-5
Paperback ISBN: 978-1-5324-1671-2
Hardcover ISBN: 978-1-5324-1672-9
Printed in the
United States of America

**Download a free eBook copy of this book using this QR code.***

or at https://xist.pub/28eb7

* Limited time only
Your name and a valid email address are required to download.
Must be redeemed by persons over 13

# Table of Contents

Guitar . . . . . . . . . . . . . . . . . . . . . . . 4

Photo Glossary . . . . . . . . . . . . 18

Things to do Next . . . . . . . . 19

Index . . . . . . . . . . . . . . . . . . . . . 20

# This is a guitar.

The guitar is a string instrument.

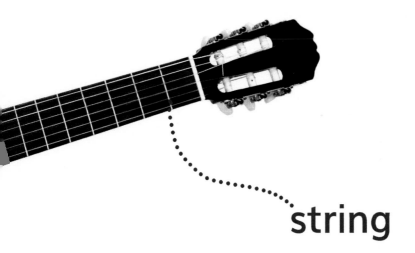

string

Guitars have six strings. Guitars are made of wood.

Pick

I play the guitar strings with my fingers or a pick.

I hold down the strings to change notes.

Guitars make many different sounds.

I can play guitar by myself.

Guitars can also be part of a band or an orchestra.

I like to play the guitar.

# Photo Glossary

## Band

group of people playing
music together

## Pick

small piece of plastic or wood
used to play a guitar

## String

the part of a musical instrument
that changes the sound

## Wood

material from a tree

# Things to do next!

## Write a Sentence

Guitars are _____.

## Drawing

Draw yourself playing a guitar.

## Sharing

Tell your classmates about a musical instrument you have heard.

# Index

band 15

instrument 6

pick 11

string 6-9, 11, 13

wood 9